this is how you know

a book of poetry

RACHEL TOALSON

Other Books by Rachel

Poetry
Life: a definition of terms
The Book of Uncommon Hours: haiku poetry
Textbook of an Ordinary Life
this is how you live

Essay
Parenthood: Has Anyone Seen My Sanity?
The Life-Changing Madness of Tidying Up After Children
This Life With Boys
We Count it All Joy: Essays
Hills I'll Probably Lie Down On

To see all the books Rachel has written, please click or visit the link below:

www.racheltoalson.com/writing

this is how you know

Published by
Batlee Press
Post Office Box 591596
San Antonio, TX 78259

Copyright ©2019 by Rachel Toalson
All rights reserved.
Printed in the United States of America.
Interior design by Toalson Media.
Cover design by Ben Toalson. www.toalsonmarketing.com

No part of this book may be reproduced or transmitted in any form or by any means, electronic or mechanical, including photocopying and recording, or by any information storage and retrieval system, without permission in writing from the publisher. For information regarding permission, write to Batlee Press, PO Box 591596, San Antonio, TX 78259.

The author appreciates your taking the time to read her work. Please consider leaving a review wherever you bought it and telling your friends how much you enjoyed it. Both of those help get the book into the hands of new readers, which is incredibly important for authors. Thank you for your support.
www.racheltoalson.com

Names: Toalson, Rachel, author.
Title: This is how you know / Rachel Toalson
Description: Second edition. | Batlee Press, Texas:
Batlee Press Books, 2019

10 9 8 7 6 5 4 3 2

First Edition—2016
Second Edition—2019

*To those who have
lost the thread of
who they are.
Remember:
You are loved.*

Introduction

I read poetry all the time. Poetry is one of those forms of writing that makes any writer better, and I try to read classic and contemporary poets every day. This has made me fall in love with poetry. Falling in love with poetry has made me want to write poetry, and I've written poetry for as long as I can remember. I think the essence of life is poetry, and so shaping that essence into my own poems is necessary for me.

My poetry typically finds its way into songs, but earlier this year we moved into an especially challenging season of life. I lost my job the same month we had our sixth child, we weren't really sure if we were supposed to move or stay put, we were drowning in all the kid responsibilities. All that and more. I didn't feel like I could open up to many people about this very personal struggle, because, in a way, it felt like a failure. So I captured all of that struggle and pain and failure and victory onto a page that became two pages and then four pages and then twenty. I wrote for three months, every day, and at the end of those three months, I had an unexpected book of poetry.

During that three-month period I met new friends and braved criticism and tried to get my kids to stay in their beds, and I felt annoyed and angry and wild and hopeful and hopeless and unsatisfied and content. All of those emotions are captured in this book of poetry.

I called the book *This is How You Know* after a poem I wrote one night when I felt especially adored by my husband.

My favorite poem is W.H. Auden's "In Memory of W.B. Yeats." I still remember the day I read this poem for the first time. It was several years ago. I was in the middle of doing some intense forgiveness work, the kind that makes your head and heart hurt. His beautiful verses changed my whole perspective. He writes: "Follow, poet, follow right to the bottom of the night, with your unconstraining voice still persuade us to rejoice; with the farming of a verse make a vineyard of the curse, sing of human unsuccess in a rapture of distress; in the deserts of the heart let the healing fountain start, in the prison of his days teach the free man how to praise."

I still get chills when I read this poem. Auden's words, written before I was even born, have the power to reach across decades and change a life for better. I learned that I could choose to turn my curses into vineyards, that my mind and my pen could trace a world of hurt and flip it around into something good and beautiful.

When I thought about recording all of my daily life poems about the ups and downs of my life, the annoying things my kids do, my relationship with my husband, I wondered at first if anyone would really be all that interested. But something I've learned in my years of writing is that when we read an essay or a story or a poem, we will always find a piece of ourselves in it. Mostly because we get to interpret it through our own eyes and our own experience. So when I went back and looked at those poems I'd scribbled in a notebook I thought no on would ever see, I considered how they would resonate with normal people in their everyday lives, too.

Sometimes we think that the life we're living is so unique and unusual, and it's true that our circumstances and the people in our lives and our reactions to our relationships and events around us are all unique. But, underneath all that, we are more alike than we know. We find ourselves in each other.

I hope that when you read *This is How You Know,* you will find a piece of yourself. I hope you'll feel less alone. I hope you'll know that while our roads may look a thousand times different, we are, deep down, the same. Just humans trying to love well and find community and live this one life for the greatest good.

how to be

1.

they will tell you
who you should be
what you should do
how to be someone
they all like
someone the world
accepts
someone who
won't cause
problems
inconvenience
challenge

they will tell you
how to be successful
and why their dream
is so much better
than your own

don't listen

walk your own way
forge your own path
be kind
hold courage

keep dreaming

this is how
to be you

2.

unmask
let them see
the real you
unadorned
bare-faced
as you are

take a picture
send it out
to the world

this is how
to be brave

3.

don't cry
don't feel
don't talk
don't give
your heart away
completely

don't serve
your family
but lead with
authority
power
force

shut up
lock away
never be free
completely

make money
forget those old dreams
now there is
responsibility

grow up

suck it up
just do what
everyone expects

pretend hide forget
completely

this is how
to be a man

4.

open up
let us in
we want to see you
cry when you need
don't hide
think for yourself

feel what you feel
know what you know
be who you want to be
even when it's not
who they want
you to be

live true
live free
live whole

forget all the success
and rules
and conventions
and lead a family
into a new
definition of success

this is how
to really be a man

5.

don't speak too loudly
don't disturb
don't argue
don't assert yourself
let them do
what they will do
shake it off
let it be
pretend it
doesn't matter

play the part
make the grade
dress for success
by which we mean
show us your skin
and make sure
you're perfect
always perfect
forever perfect

this is how
to be a woman

6.

take off your makeup
let down your hair
take a good look
at your naked face
in the mirror
and smile

stand tall without
the whole world
on your shoulders
believe in beauty
and know
you are

beautiful

say what you mean
in your own voice
in your own language
don't let them tell you
who to be
or what to look like
or how to live

choose for yourself

and then stand strong
proud
true

this is how
to be a real woman.

7.

open wide
say it out loud
that thing
that thing you
that thing you probably
shouldn't say
out loud

but do

let them see those
locked-away pieces
let them help
in their own way

brave the invasion

invite them in
where you don't
often invite others

this is how
to be known

8.

how does it look
everything perfect
at least on the outside

rocks left alone
porch chairs just so
don't do this
don't do that
stay off my grass
leave me alone

don't touch
don't look
don't talk

this is how
to be neighborly

9.

family of three
family of eight
we don't have
much in common
and yet we do
but we will never know
unless we break bread
and commune
and get to know
and love

so fling wide the doors
break bread
around the same table
make the house messy
dishes piled high
dessert spilled on the floor
wine tipped over
by a gesturing hand

stay for a while
at least until
the stars wink

come

sit
eat
together

this is how
to really be neighborly

10.

fancy cars
more than one
shining out front
more rooms than
you'll ever fill
and another five
in a house tucked
in the woods
or on the beach
or standing tall
in the city
for when vacation
comes calling

money stacked high
but not for long
because there is always
a new boat
an expensive car
another wardrobe
waiting to
make you happy

work, work, work
to fill a bank

so you can
buy, buy, buy
because a bank
full of money
is what you need
to say you've
made it

this is how
to be successful

11.

there are choices
we will have to make
promotion or no
job or no
family or work

and the one
that matters
is the one that
will shape
who we become

what is right
what is wrong
which one
makes us fuller
better
greater

what we do
who we are
who we will
yet become
in the deepest
spaces of our heart

choosing full life
over full bank account

this is how
to really be successful

12.

freedom of speech
does not grant you
the right to forget
who you are
who I am
who we are

freedom of speech
does not grant you
the right to hurt me
in the places
one can't see

freedom of speech
does not grant you
the right to
lash out
diminish
tear down

there is responsibility
that comes with
freedom of speech
it must be used wisely
it is no excuse

it is no justification
it is no reason
for filthy words
that attack another

take care with words
take care with hearts
add to the conversation
without detracting
from the dignity
of another

we belong
to each other
remember that

this is how
to be human

how to parent

13.

barging in
because he hasn't
seen you all day
and he can't wait
to show what
he got at school

look up
listen to hear
show him love
with interest
no matter how long
he takes
to tell it

this is how
you love a son

14.

watch them play
having fun
like they never
get to at home
because life is busy

stay up late
fudge on bedtime
let them eat
whatever they want
bend the rules
in the name of life

wish the weekend
would last forever
but not quite

this is how
you do vacation

15.

watch and wait
it's coming
see them
hit kick punch
feel the anger of it
torch your insides

but take a deep breath
and talk and console
and suggest how
to do better next time
because you know
there will be
a next time

forgive
and give them
a chance to
make it right

this is how
you teach a child

16.

books on the floor
books in a chair
books all around

stretch out
on the floor
let the kids
climb on a back
no matter
how weary

get those accents
ready
all the acting
cued up
voice prepped
for action

and then
the giggles begin
woven around story
and knowledge
and magic

this is how

to read to your children

17.

roll those superhero socks
into a superhero cup
spread that spider
across a wide wall
and hook the
pipe cleaner legs
all across

spend the morning baking
that cookie cake
with a white web
lining it

decorate
and set up
food games presents

and then
breathe
watch
enjoy

this is how you
do a birthday

18.

lose your cool
strike out
with words
and maybe hands

say exactly what
you're thinking
that this is just
too hard
that they are just
too hard
that you wish
they would be
different

then believe it

this is how
you begin to resent
a child

19.

watch him get
the reading award
a gold medal
that hangs his neck

watch him beam
watch him walk proud
watch him shine

and then listen
to those words
how he tried to give
his medal to
someone who
didn't have one
and feel your
heart swell
feel the jolt
of that purity
feel the story
it tells

this is how
you see their future

20.

choose the right words
honor their hearts
speak in gentle tones
instead of harsh ones
and watch them unfold
blossom
grow

in the light
of understanding
show them who
you want them to be
in who you are

this is how
you train up a child
in the way
he should go

21.

keep getting out of bed
keep knocking on
a bedroom door
keep talking past
lights out

keep wrestling
keep yelling
keep calling out
for something more
always something more

this is how
you annoy
your parents

22.

sit for a while
open the conversation
ask about his day
his friends
the bartering project
he finished at school

watch him bloom
because of a question
because he gets to
talk about art
and trade
and a new book
with someone
who cares

listen, feel, see
the young man
he will one day be

this is how
you fill a son's heart

23.

sit in a dark room
type away
while kids are out
swimming and playing
and you are here
missing and writing

feel the absence
wrap your neck
and look for your baby
one smile and
you can get
three more paragraphs
down

and then they come
piling through the door
laughing, jostling, shouting
shut off the glow
because it can wait
but this moment cannot

and later
when they are
tucked in bed

when you have gotten over
that missing
race toward
the deadline again

this is how
you work when
you're a parent

24.

lie in shadows
with music singing
around chairs
around people
around you

let that music move
your pen
while kids play
in the nursery
down the hall

take the moments
and use what you can
yet remain present
for the most
important parts

stop, start, stop, start
summon flow
in the tiny spaces

this is how
you learn to be
a writer mama

25.

stolen moments
one here, one there
locked in a bathroom
for five minutes
of peace
with a book
of course

standing in the
pickup line
nose buried
eyes racing
to beat the bell

listening to audio
while nursing
the baby

read to them
read with them
read for them

a page a day
is still a page a day

this is how
to read when
you're a mother

26.

it's time for sleep
and yet they come
again
one by one
to say goodnight
to give a kiss
to hug

and even though
you're tired
even though you're done
even though they
should be in bed
dream dancing
you let them come
because it's them
and you
and a language
that needs no
other words

this is how
boys love a mama

how to love

27.

an arm wrapped
around shoulders
or wrapped around
a waist
carrying the hurt one
out the door
loading up
leaving all
the work behind
at the drop of a foot

an ear turned
to a lover's call
a cry for help
even if it
isn't the first

a sandwich made
in the busy
a water bottle
filled by the bed

time carved out
to tend to a
lover's list

even though hours
are too short

the rumble of breath
in the dead of night
comforting in its
familiarity

words whispered
in an ear
cutting through sleep
and warming
the one they meet

a book saved
from a plastic bag
and given during
need
a foot rub
or scalp massage
when sleep is
what's needed
but it just won't
come

a kiss
on the mouth

light and soft
and lovely
stolen in all
the silent moments
a flutter deep down
in the same place
it was all those
years before

this is how
you know

28.

five minute checkins
tag-teaming to bedtime
open communication
on nights kids
actually go to sleep
before your bedtime

a kiss every time
you leave the house
and when you return
some longer than others

a locked door
the nights you just
need time alone
without guilt
clinging to the sheets

dishes done for one
notes left for another
because you love
differently

staying on the same side
no matter what

engaging arguments
that don't always resolve
but knowing you're not
going anywhere

choosing good assumptions
choosing forgiveness
choosing love

falling into bed
at the end of a long day
with arms that
wrap and hold
and set the world
right again

weekends away
just the two of you
so you remember why
you fell in love
in the first place

this is how
you stay married
after children

29.

lie in bed
talking of life
and dreams
and all those things
the minutes
hardly see anymore

lock the door
so they can't
get in again

hold hands
turn off screens
cry, laugh, sing

look into the eyes
of your always-love
and just for once
be still

no business
no home-talk
no kid questions
just each other

now breathe

because it won't
last forever
these pseudo-dates

fall asleep together
because kids are
sure to be up
bright and early
tomorrow

this is how
you have a date
at home

30.

watch him look
watch him
try to impress
because there's
someone watching

watch him wish
he could be
someone different

but you're wrong

this is how
you invent something
that doesn't exist

31.

keep score
one against the other
confuse what's fair
with what's equal
and bring it all back
every time selfishness
comes knocking

kick where it hurts
fling guilt in a face
count the damage
watch it twist a love
and then wonder
what went wrong

it all went wrong
every single bit
love, hate, regret

this is how
you tear a marriage
in two

32.

yell and rage
and be someone
you're not
deep down

see the same look
on their faces
fear mixed with
sadness
and feel your
sadness too

but keep going
let the words fly
until everyone gets quiet
so quiet
and the whole world
sits on a pyre

then step aside
fling the final match
and watch it burn

this is how
you torch relationships

33.

remember all you've done
for so many years
remember the dreams
you gave up
the sacrifices you made
the unhappiness you felt
stuck in a job
that led nowhere
feel the rage
the disappointment
the surprising weight
of it
and do nothing
say nothing
try nothing

and then
when they least
expect it
throw it back
remind the one
who hasn't done
as much
that he hasn't
done as much

remember how now
you might have to
do it all again
back to shackles
when you have
tasted freedom

and grieve
alone

this is how
you give the bitter root
a hold

34.

nod your head
pretend you hear
and keep up the charade
every time she
opens her mouth

go through the
motions of listening
and make her think
you really are
because there are
more important people
talking in your life

especially your phone

you're really good
really smooth
really convincing

and then when
she asks if you've heard
stumble, mumble
try to recover
but she'll find

you out

a woman
always knows

say you're sorry
but don't make
much effort to change
or do better
or listen to hear

until

this is how
you lose her

35.

sit beside her
don't say much
about anything
especially not babies

except that
you have a
new one
and she is
trying for one
has been trying
for too long

but don't ask
about it
or try to say
anything sure
about the future
because you just
don't know

you just don't know

you have so many
she lost the two

and what is there
to say

except you love her
and you hope for her
and that her
mother heart is
large and lovely
and that's all

that's enough

this is how
you heal a sister

36.

see the ones
you haven't seen
in a year
because you have
other responsibilities
other family
other more important
things to do

say something
about her son
the one you don't know
at all
but only see
once every three years
and feel the rift
grow deeper
wider
longer

keep it up
on and on
and on again

this is how

you make her
go for good

37.

forget their name
ask what they do
talk about nothing
or all the wrong things

try to be someone
you're not
play a good part
the one they want
you to play

this is how
you meet someone new

38.

exchange names
talk about what
really matters
dreams, hurts,
disappointments
the way you work
a job you hate
how you wish
you could have
children
why you can't wait
to get out of here
and what you
hope to do next

leave small talk
superficial talk
shallow talk
at the door

this is how
you meet someone new
and make a friend

39.

I am an artist
I create
for the world
for you
for free

please
value what I do
see what it's worth
dip your hand
in my well
and then appreciate
the beauty
instead of
taking, taking, taking
expecting what
isn't really yours

an artist gives
but that
does not mean
you deserve
what they give

so let them know

what their words
their pictures
their songs
have meant to you
and give them back
your open hands

this is how
you love an artist

how to live

40.

fist clenched
lungs full
releasing breath
cry
life

new and bright
pink and wrinkled
eyes glazed
and thick
puffy around
the edges
but still
seeing everything

you never thought
to imagine
cold and light
and hands
prodding
poking
lifting

and then
you rest in

the arms of
the most beautiful
person you've
ever met

this is how
you come into
the world

41.

time goes by
you walk
run
skip
everything still new
and brilliant

fists unclench a little
trust opens them
one finger
at a time
a whole world
of possibility
there before you
and you will need
open hands
to grasp it

learning doing being
walking more deeply
into who you are
unapologetic about
what you do
and say
and dream

this is how
you grow

42.

listen to hear
watch to see
look it up
if you don't
understand

find out what
you don't know
always keep looking
for ways to
be better
do better
understand better

this is how
you learn
something new

43.

write out that schedule
revise it when
the season ends
and a new one begins

repeat and
repeat and
repeat
and never get
so fixed on one way
that another way
seems impossible
or wrong

fluid, not right
grey, not black and white
spirit, not law

this is how
you adapt

44.

find a corner
sit in a chair
hold a baby
so he can see
all the ones
you don't know

let him talk
where you can't

listen to the
conversations
around you
but keep your peace
endure for them
and find one
who might make
a good conversation
partner

this is how
you survive a party

45.

the sugar calls
sitting in the fridge
that icing from
a boy's birthday
left over from
the cake

just a little taste
just a finger
dipped and cleaned
just one…

don't open the fridge
don't even go near
except you need
something to eat
something from here
so…

open

look see remember
how sweet it was
remember how smooth
remember how good

just one little taste
come on
it won't hurt you
just one

open the lid
it's okay
it's just one

no no no
no I won't

it won't ruin you

yes it will
I know how
this works

open the lid

stop stop stop

dip the finger

don't do it

taste
eat
binge

this is how
you cave

46.

one day
at a time
one hour
at a time
one minute
at a time

you only have to
say no this minute
this hour
this day

keep the bad stuff
off your shelves
out of pantries
away from here
don't ever risk
letting them talk
luring you in
breaking your resolve

say no this minute
this hour
this day
but just

this minute

this is how
you change
your diet lifestyle

47.

listen to them talk
look at their art
read words
find stories
they're all so good
so put together
so desired
and creative
and sharp

and even though
they're meant
to be inspiring
what you do
is compare
one life to another
theirs so far
above this one
you have

and somehow you feel
diminished
overlooked
unworthy
like the world

could not hold space
for the both of you
like you will
never be known
for great

let their successes
stop you

this is how
you get lost

48.

know who you are
know what you love
know the world
needs it

then do it

this is how
you get found

49.

as fast as you can
as hard as you can
as strong as you can

lift one
plant another
over and over
and over again
in soft and gentle
and hard and strong
rhythm

breath stinging
burning through lungs
that barely
remember normal

feet clapping
heart snapping
ideas flapping

this is how
you run

50.

let the music
swell around you
let it lift
and carry you
toward a better place
a healing place

let it whisper
what you know
but cannot
see right now

let it blink
all around
and before
and behind

this is how
you rest

51.

read a book
or not
talk about a book
or not
it doesn't really matter

gather with them
share about life
open up so wide
you cry and wonder
if you've said too much
or not enough

let them walk you
back to hope

wave goodbye
until next time

this is how
you run a book club

52.

you have such a hard time
with your 3-year-old
well just wait until
he's eight

yeah, and then
wait until he's twelve
thirteen
fifteen
eighteen

I have it harder
than you
believe me

those were the
easy
simpler
better days
so stop your
complaining

motherhood is mostly easy
except for my kind
believe me

my kid never
did that
must be bad parenting

be a parent
and then it won't
be so hard
believe me

this is how
you start a
parenting war

53.

remember those days
you felt like the stage
would never end
all that work
from dawn until midnight
recall how exhausting
it was

empathize, feel what
they're feeling
acknowledge that it's hard
and it gets harder
but you get better
along with the hard

pat them on the back
for the work
they're doing
in their own season

this is how
you quell a parenting war

54.

let her rest
read
sleep
plan
like she never
gets to do
when she's "on"

let her take off
let her listen
to the rain
and the sounds
of memories made

ask for nothing
today of all days

this is how
you love a mother

55.

wish you could have
been there
wish there was
a way
wish you could have
seen him play
on the field trip
you said
you'd never miss

wish you could
turn back time

this is how
you let regret win

56.

get your hopes up
and feel them
fall flat

maybe it will work
maybe not
maybe struggle
is all you'll
ever get
maybe giving up
would just be easier

it always is

but you'll pull through
you'll keep going
you'll figure it out

you know
it's who you are

this is how
you keep swinging

57.

lean in
to the strong ones
hear their voice
feel their hands
let them walk you
back from the edge
out from the dark
into the light

lean in
and fall into the arms
that will hold

this is how
you find brave

58.

the crowded room
everyone is talking
caught in conversation
that means something
at least for them

and yet there is
so much inside
that waits to be said

there is no one
to talk to
in this room
filled with people

so you sit alone
breaking, reeling
and no one
even knows

this is how
you let loneliness win

59.

get so angry
fling hasty words
toward the one
who hurt you most
at least today
and hurl those swings
every which way
until someone else
gets hurt
because you're hurt
and they should
be hurt

and then
regret
cry
scream

this is how
you lose

60.

melody rising
weaving in and out
of harmony
up down
and around the sides
no note left untouched
at least not the ones
that are important
for this song
this moment
this heart

lift and lower
swell and fade
like a lover
lost in a moment

this is how
you make music

61.

it only takes a second
of letting your guard down
of not paying attention
of letting hurry
rule the day

and then you're falling
breaking
rolling
down on the floor
barely breathing
and six weeks
of limping
resting
asking for help
is the only remedy

this is how
you learn to leave
hurry at the
top of the stairs

62.

the sadness waits
in the shadows
of a crowded room

you try to
put on that face
everyone is
comfortable with
even though you
are one step away
from breaking apart
but you hide it well
and carry on
your lonely life
and no one thinks
to ask

because of course
you are happy
and of course
you are well
and of course
your heart still beats
in the same direction
it always did

there is so much
they won't know
just by looking

there is so much
you won't get
the chance to say

this is how
you wither
in the hands of life

63.

feel the overwhelm

the way it can hit
when you least
expect it
the way it can
knock you
off your feet
the way it can
break you
wrap around you
put you back together
with all the wrong parts

feel the overwhelm

let its wave
crash and burn
and push and pull you
toward action
toward solution
toward manic planning

feel the overwhelm

take out the
white boards (again)
scribble down words
that look like answers
if you look
just right

and then move on
.

this is how
you keep hope alive

64.

high
low
every day different
it's this trying season
this insecurity
this not knowing
where we'll be
next month
or next year

a heart can't live
in a wrinkling place

so it begins
to shrivel
and shrink
inside

a person needs
stability
security
a little control
but this life
is nothing
like that

stop dwelling
on what you
don't have

keep hoping
keep dreaming
keep trying

this is how
you don't stop
believing

65.

stay up too late
talking with friends
sharing it all
the good, the bad
the ugly

and they don't
turn away
they don't correct
they don't run
the other way

no
they stand strong
where you are weak
and so you are
all made strong
together

this is how
you get back up
when you're down

66.

the deadline is here
that end-of-month
reconciling day
and it's been
so long since
you've felt ready

but time doesn't stop
it flies on
and now you
sit with a calculator
and a slim line
of hope

will it be enough

this is how
you end the month

67.

worry, stress
try to find
your own way
figure it out
be okay

take any job
that comes
watch what you thought
what you hoped
what you dreamed
turn into just
one more
disappointment

turn it inside out
and upside down
and all the way
back again
and then
just forget to
breathe

this is how
you lose a day

of your life

68.

all these years
you've given back
lost all these
pieces of yourself
in the name of
something bigger

and in your
time of need
there is no
safety net
no room for help
no taking care
of you
or yours

and it's not
that you expected
anything in return
but there are
promises
fail-safes
guarantees of a kind
but it didn't work
for you

and now there is
no opportunity
to share
or ask
or seek help

a heart can
turn harder
than stone
when you're
not looking
because of these
promises that
just weren't meant
for you
(at least that's
what it feels like)

it doesn't take long
for a heart
to give up hope
but you try
to keep going
carry on
just get through
with your self-respect
still intact

this is how
you start to break
in secret

69.

tell them just
what they could do
if they had
the courage

tell them the world
needs their art
their presence
their contribution

tell them it's scary
that you've been there
that fear never
really goes away

tell them you
are in their corner

this is how
you encourage
a fellow artist

70.

visit goals
bounce ideas
off each other
dream out loud

map out stories
plan whole weeks
evaluate strategy

identify priorities
learn more
uncover the path
to dreams

write it all
on a white board
snap a picture
like a snapshot
of life

don't steal the thunder

lift up
celebrate
the differences

and support another
with no thought
of what you
might get back

this is how
you collaborate

71.

make the call
mark it off
the to-do list
where it's been
sitting for weeks

pick up the phone
make the arrangements
and then it's done

this is how
you clear space
in your brain
in your life
in your heart
for what really matters

72.

dig through the past
and find the holes
open them wide
and look within
try to make sense
of what's living there
and start the journey
of exploration
of healing
of repairing
all the broken pieces
restoring what was lost
walking deeper
into the truth

and live to tell
the story

this is how
you break free

73.

strap it on
string your fingers
pluck until it sings
and you sing along

this is how
you become music

74.

bite off more
than you can chew
speaking here
writing there
making goals that
seem possible
until you remember
how short time is

try to do it all
keep house
raise kids
work the successful
full-time career
host the friends
cook the meals
make the bed
mow the lawn
weed the garden
wash the dishes
sort the loads
fill the fridge
turn out the lights

make sure you're there

don't miss a thing
sign papers
build relationships
make it all
look easy
simple
perfect

this is how
you feel overwhelmed

75.

when they ask
silly personal
none-of-your-business
questions
smile at them
and answer kindly

then look around
and be glad
for your large family

this is how
you beat them
at their shame game

76.

there is a moment
just before you
take a fall
when you wish
you could take it back
turn back time
slow it down
and just start over

but you see it happening
and there is no way
to stop it
you hear it happening
and there is no way
to stop it
you feel it happening
and there is no way
to stop it

time does not
work in reverse
so think
slow down
see
while you still can

this is how
you avoid the fall

77.

plan your course
plot your direction
sail away on
uncharted waters
of your own making

steer
balance
overcommit
then feel unmoored
so

hit the drawing board
clear the way
take a closer look
narrow down
to broaden out

learn to do
the most right thing
instead of all the things

save the rest
for later

this is how
you reset your life

78.

something is wrong
neck tilted
not normal
look it up
compare notes
try to figure
it out yourself
study his symptoms
and forget
you're not the doctor

try to fix it

worry, stress, blow up
can't think
can't move
can't even say
what it is exactly
feel the cellophane
wrap your
neck throat mouth
and clamp tight
then try to breathe
just try to breathe
come on, breathe

try to survive it

ice climbs
higher deeper wider
until you cannot
control that mind
and where it lands

this is how
anxiety steals
an afternoon

79.

why can't we
just share
our art
with the world

why does it
have to be
a cultural war

why is it
your art
my art
when it could be
our art

this is how
not to be
an artist community

80.

make a plan
stick to it
squeeze the
seconds
minutes
hours
marking them off
line by line
task by task

yet still take time
to kiss
and love
and delight in
the ones
who brighten
your life

this is how
you seize a day

81.

the artist within
can show you
what life is

let her out

this is how
you fly

82.

watch to see
listen to hear
touch to know

stay here in
this moment
instead of there
in your mind
constantly planning
what's next

this is how
you live

the end

About the Author

Life is a great poem.
You don't have to look far
to find the way words crowd
around each other.
Rachel will sit out on her back porch
while her six sons laugh
and screech and play,
and she swears it sounds like poetry.
She will walk along an old
rusted railroad track where she
played as a kid, and she will see
the purple of her son's shirt and the
white of another son's socks and the
red of her youngest son's jacket,
and she swears it looks like poetry.
Every sense engages in this dance,
taste, smell, touch, see, hear.
Poetry is all around.

Though she writes a handful of blogs
every week and pens her fiction stories
while kids are napping,
her favorite thing to write is poetry.
Because all of life is a great poem.

Her favorite poets are W.H. Auden,
Mary Oliver, Edward Hirsch,

John Keats, Shel Silverstein,
and W.B. Yeats.
She studies them daily,
because if one wants to write
good poetry, one has to read it.
www.racheltoalson.com

Enjoy more titles from Rachel Toalson

racheltoalson.com

Rachel Toalson Poetry
Starter Library

Enjoy more of Rachel Toalson's poetry with these free downloads.

To get your FREE books, visit *
RachelToalson.com/FreeBook

*Must be 13 or older to be eligible

www.ingramcontent.com/pod-product-compliance
Lightning Source LLC
Chambersburg PA
CBHW021440080526
44588CB00009B/618